Tidal Zone

John Woodward

Heinemann Library
Chicago, Illinois

Consultant: Lundie Spence, Ph.D.
Director, SouthEast Center for Ocean Sciences Education Excellence, South Carolina Sea Grant Consortium

Produced by The Brown Reference Group plc
Project Editor: Tim Harris
Sub Editor: Tom Webber
Designer: Jeni Child
Picture Researcher: Sean Hannaway
Illustrator: Mark Walker
Managing Editor: Bridget Giles

Printed in China by WKT Company Limited

08 07 06 05 04
10 9 8 7 6 5 4 3 2 1

Cataloging-in-Publication data available from Library of Congress

Woodward, John, 1954-
   Tidal zone / John Woodward.
      v. cm. -- (Exploring the oceans)
Contents: The tidal zone -- Your mission -- The moon and tides --
Mega tide -- Pulling the plug -- Rip tide -- Sea power -- Wind and waves
-- Tidal pools -- Clammed up -- On the beach -- Hidden riches -- Mud and
marsh -- Fuel stop -- Seagrass meadows -- Turtle nursery -- Mangrove
swamp -- Mangrove life -- A breeding beach -- Orca attack! -- Mission
debriefing.
   ISBN 1-4034-5128-1 (hardcover) -- ISBN 1-4034-5134-6 (pbk.)
   1. Tide pool ecology--Juvenile literature. 2. Oceanography--Juvenile
literature. [1. Tide pool ecology. 2. Tidal pools. 3. Ecology. 4.
Oceanography.] I. Title.
   QH541.5.S35W66 2004
   551.46--dc22

                                                    2003021295

Acknowledgements
The author and publishers are grateful to the following for permission
to reproduce copyright material:
Front Cover: Coral reef flat on the Great Barrier Reef, Australia. (Stuart Westmorland/Corbis).
Back Cover: Corbis: Mark A. Johnson
p.1 UNEP/Topham; p.2t George H. H. Huey/Corbis; p.2c Photolink/Photodisc, Inc; p.2b Paul A.
Souders/Corbis; p.3 Hermann Brehm/Nature Picture Library; p.4-5 Photolink/Photodisc, Inc; p.6-7
David Cayless/Oxford Scientific Films; p.8-9 Richard T. Nowitz/Corbis; p.10-11 Corbis Royalty Free;
p.12-13 Carl & Ann Purcell/Corbis; p.14-15 Adrian Warren/Ardea; p.15tr Jonathan Smith/Cordaiy
Photo Library Ltd/Corbis; p.16-17 Paul A. Souders/Corbis; p.17tr Galen Rowell/Corbis; p.18 Heather
Angel/Natural Visions; p.19 W. Cody/Corbis; p.20-21 Mark Deeble & Victoria Stone/Oxford Scientific
Films; p.21tr Stephen Krasemann/NHPA; p.22-23 Jeffrey L. Rotman/Corbis; p.23bc Tim
Edwards/Nature Picture Library; p.23tr Richard Hamilton Smith/Corbis; p.24bl GSFC/NASA; p.24-25
Farrell Grehan/Corbis; p.26 Heather Angel/Natural Visions; p.27 Jeffrey L. Rotman/Corbis; p.28-29
Heather Angel/Natural Visions; p.29tr Townsend P. Dickinson/Topham; p.30 Jim Zipp/Ardea; p.31
Tom Vezo/Nature Picture Library; p.32-33 William Boyce/Corbis; p.33cr Jeff Foott/Nature Picture
Library; p.34 Jeffrey L. Rotman/Corbis; p.35 George H. H. Huey/Corbis; p.36br Jurgen Freund/Nature
Picture Library; p.36-37 Jim Richardson/Corbis; p.38-39 Joe McDonald/Corbis; p.39br Martin
Harvey/NHPA; p.40-41 Hermann Brehm/Nature Picture Library; p.42-43 Jeff Foott/Nature Picture
Library; p.43tr Jeff Foott/Nature Picture Library; p.44 Pat O'Hara/Corbis.

Some words are shown in bold, **like this.** You can find out what they mean by looking in the glossary.

Contents

The Tidal Zone

Oceans are sometimes violent, dangerous places. Thousands of sailors have died while trying to cross them. Yet the roughest part of any ocean is not its center. There, huge waves roll over water that is miles deep. The most violent part is where the sea first meets the land.

This is where great waves smash against the rocks of continents. Waves can break rocks like explosives. Rushing water creates deadly **whirlpools.** And the shallow sea often hides sharp **reefs** and dangerous sandbanks. Such places are littered with the wrecks of ships. They crossed oceans but sunk within sight of land.

But this area is not just dangerous for ships and sailors. It is dangerous for wildlife, too.

Only the toughest can survive the constant pounding of the waves. And there is another problem. Every day the sea level rises and falls as ocean water is pulled by the Moon's **gravity.** This up-and-down movement is called the **tides.** Since the shore slopes, an up-and-down movement of the ocean makes a back-and-forth flow of the tides. Tides can cover large areas of shore with water, then expose them again just a few hours later. Dry land becomes a shallow seafloor, then dry land again. This is the tidal zone.

Highs and lows

The tidal zone starts at the highest point on the shore that is covered at high tide. It ends at the lowest point that is uncovered at low tide. Breaking waves splash sea water on land above the high tide mark. This area is called the **splash zone.**

Sometimes, the tide level rises higher than usual. Then it sinks lower than usual. So, more of the shore is affected by the tides. These are called spring tides. They have nothing to do with the spring season. At other times, the water level rises and falls less than usual. This makes neap tides.

During a neap tide, the lowest parts of the tidal zone stay underwater all the time, and the highest parts stay dry.

So, some parts of the tidal zone are covered by water much longer than others. This affects the types of things that can live there. The type of shore also affects the things that live there. Exposed, rocky shores and quiet, sandy or muddy shores make life difficult for living things in quite different ways. So, different **organisms** live on different shores.

Why do animals and plants live in the tidal zone, if life is so difficult? It is because the water near the shore is rich in food. Anything living there will do well, provided it is tough enough to survive.

These powerful waves are crashing in the tidal zone. The waves were whipped up by strong winds in the open ocean.

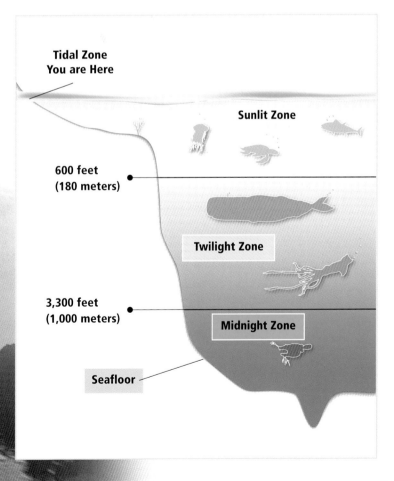

Tidal Zone
You are Here

Sunlit Zone

600 feet
(180 meters)

Twilight Zone

3,300 feet
(1,000 meters)

Midnight Zone

Seafloor

Your Mission

This sandy beach is part of the tidal zone. The lines are ripples of sand made by waves when the tide was higher.

The three parts of the tidal zone

The tidal zone is divided into three parts: the lower shore, middle shore, and upper shore. The lower shore is only exposed by very low tides. Some days it is underwater all day.

The middle shore is covered by water and then exposed to the air every day. The upper shore is only covered by the highest tides. Some days it is not underwater at all.

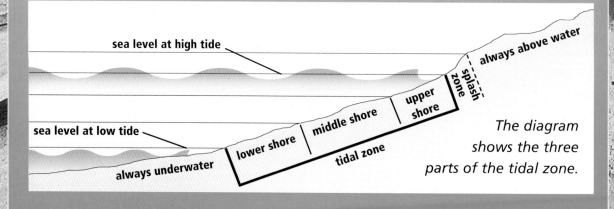

sea level at high tide

always above water

splash zone

upper shore

sea level at low tide

lower shore   middle shore

tidal zone

always underwater

The diagram shows the three parts of the tidal zone.

You are going to find out about the tidal zone and the things that live there. The first place you visit will be the Bay of Fundy in Canada. It has the biggest **tides** in the world. Then you will investigate the rocky shores of California, on the west coast, before heading east to explore the sandy beaches and **salt marshes** of Cape Cod. There, you learn how the beaches and marshes support millions of animals and shorebirds.

Then you follow the Atlantic coast to the Caribbean Sea. Here, the water is warmer, and the shore life is very different. You swim with manatees over the seagrass meadows of a Caribbean island. Later, you will watch sea turtles as they come ashore to lay their eggs on the beaches of Suriname in South America.

After this your journey takes you to the weird world of a tropical mangrove swamp. There, you see how the forest can spread into the ocean and live in airless, waterlogged mud. The final stop on this voyage of exploration is the Valdés Peninsula, in Argentina. Seals and even whales make use of tidal shores, there. And you get to watch them. Enjoy the trip.

Arctic Ocean

North America

Europe

Asia

Pacific Ocean

Africa

equator

South America

Atlantic Ocean

Indian Ocean

Australia

1
2
3
4
5
6
7

Places you will visit
1. Bay of Fundy
2. Gulf of Maine
3. California
4. Cape Cod
5. Caribbean island
6. Suriname
7. Valdés Peninsula

The Moon and Tides

Low tide in a harbor often leaves most boats stranded. In a few hours high tide will fill the harbor, and the boats will float again.

It is a bright summer afternoon on the coast of Nova Scotia, in eastern Canada. You have come to a small harbor on the rocky Atlantic shore to hire a boat. When you arrived five hours ago, you saw the boat tied up to the dock. You stepped aboard to see the skipper, but found a note saying he would be back after lunch. So you went off to buy some supplies. Now you are back, but the boat has gone.

Or has it? When you go to the dock to look, you find that most of the water in the harbor has drained away. The boat is still there, but it is now sitting on the mud, way below you. It was hidden by the dock wall. You now have to climb down a ladder to get to it.

On the way down, you notice that the exposed dock wall is covered with sea life. Near the top there are thousands of small, gray, cone-shaped shells called barnacles. A little farther down there are bigger cone-shaped shells called limpets. Then there are clumps of seaweed and clusters of blue-black mussels. They have all been left high and dry by the falling **tide.**

Up and down

Why does the tide rise and fall? It all has to do with the Moon. The Moon travels around Earth in an **orbit** that takes 24 hours and 50 minutes, or just more than a day. The Moon's **gravity** pulls the ocean water into a slight oval, a bit like a football. One bulge faces the Moon and the other faces away. As it circles Earth, the Moon drags these bulges of water around with it. When a bulge moves into your part of the world, the tide rises. As it moves away, the tide falls again.

Why we have spring tides

When the Moon is on the same side of Earth as the Sun (that is the time of a new Moon), or the opposite side (the time of a full Moon), the gravities of the Moon and the Sun work together. That makes extra-big spring tides. But when the Moon is out to the side of Earth, their gravities work against each other to cause much smaller neap tides. Spring tides have nothing to do with the spring season.

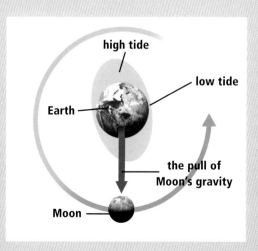

This diagram shows how the tides work.

Mega Tide

It is a while before you find the skipper of the boat and load your gear on board. The **tide** has started to rise again. The Moon causes two high tides every day in most places. So, the next high tide will be about 12 hours after the last one. Since there is a low tide between each high tide, the water level will take about six hours to rise from low to high. It was 3 o'clock in the afternoon when you found the boat sitting on the mud. It should be high tide at about 9 o'clock in the evening.

But you do not need to wait that long. By 5 o'clock, the water is deep enough and the boat is afloat. So your skipper sets off. You have a long trip ahead of you—about 200 miles (320 kilometers). You are going into the Bay of Fundy, which is between Nova Scotia and New Brunswick. Luckily it is a fast boat, so you might make the trip in about 10 hours. But the skipper is going to anchor on the way. You will soon find out why.

Going with the flow

The Bay of Fundy has the biggest **tide range** in the world. In the Minas Basin, at its eastern end, the water level can rise by as much as 45 feet (14 meters) in six hours. That is the height of a five-story building! These huge tides are caused

by the way masses of Atlantic water push into the Gulf of Maine and are forced into the Bay of Fundy.

When a tide leaves the shore it is called the ebb tide. As the ebb tide pours out of the Bay of Fundy, the powerful **tidal stream** flows at more than 9 miles an hour (14 kilometers an hour). That may not sound a lot, but trying to motor against it in a small boat is tough. So your skipper anchors the boat at about 10:30 at night. Then the ebb tide is against you.

You both get some sleep. When the tide starts to rise at 3:30 in the morning the skipper gets going again. You are lucky: you can carry on sleeping.

When you get up, the boat is moving fast. That is because the flood tide is carrying it along faster than the engines alone would be able to. Two hours later, you race past Cape Split in the Minas Channel. Then the skipper heads for port. You step on to the dock at 9:45 in the morning. It is just before high tide.

A very low tide in the Bay of Fundy has uncovered a wide beach and caves. When the tide is high, the beach and caves are hidden underwater.

Places you will visit
1. Bay of Fundy
2. Gulf of Maine
3. California
4. Cape Cod

Greenland

North America

Pacific Ocean

North Atlantic Ocean

1

3

4

2

Pulling the Plug

Not long after you arrive, the **tide** starts to fall again. It is as if someone pulled the plug from a giant bathtub. The water drains away, exposing **tidal flats** that gleam in the summer sunshine. Many thousands of shorebirds pick their way over the mud and sand. They are looking for food. After breakfast you pack your bag and follow them out.

There is a gentle slope from the shore down across the tidal flats. When you reach the waterline, the sea has not gone out too far. The water is surprisingly warm in the shallows. You check the temperature with a thermometer. Then you check the saltiness of the water with a **salometer.** It is more salty than you expected. This is because the warm seawater **evaporates** (turns to water vapor) quicker than colder

When the tide is very low, you can see how the tidal flats gently rise and fall. There are shallow, salty pools in the lowest areas. When the tide rises again, the whole area will be flooded once more.

sea water. When water evaporates, it leaves its salt behind. This makes the water that is left even saltier.

High and dry

As the water drains away faster and faster, you follow the tide out farther. When you look back after three hours, you see that the boat is high and dry. It is well above the level of your head because of the slope. It is hard to believe that you arrived in port when the water was deep. The whole area is now a huge muddy beach. Winding channels carry water off the land. When you check the water this far out you find that it is colder and not so salty. Out here the flats do not have as long to warm up under the Sun. The rising tide covers them before they have a chance to warm up. At high tide the water also gets deeper here. Deeper water does not warm up as fast as shallow water.

Eventually you decide to turn back. According to your tide table it will be another two hours before the tide stops going out. It is already a long walk back to the boat, and you want your lunch.

Tide tables

If the Moon orbited Earth in exactly 24 hours, the times of high and low tide would be the same every day. But since it takes 24 hours and 50 minutes, the times of high and low tide change every day. You can find them in special tide tables, which are different for every stretch of coast.

NOVEMBER 2003 MONTEREY BAY TIDE TABLES					
		Low Tide		High Tide	
		Sunrise 6:26 PDT		Sunset 5:00 pm PDT	
Date	Day	AM-Ht.	PM-Ht.	AM-Ht.	PM-Ht.
1	SA	10:32 am 3.1	11:23 pm 0.1	5:46 am 4.3	3:57 pm 4.9
2	SU	11.55 am 2.7	....	6:32 am 4.6	5.19 pm 4.6
3	M	12:16 am 0.2	12:57 pm 2.1	7:10 am 4.8	6:30 pm 4.5
4	TU	1:02 am 0.5	1:48 pm 1.6	7:42 am 0.5	7:31 pm 4.4
5	W	1:40 am 0.9	2:31 pm 1.1	8:09 am 5.2	8:25 pm 4.3

A tide table shows when the tide is high and when it is low. It also shows how high and low the water goes.

Rip Tide

The skipper of your boat takes care to read the **tide** tables. If he did not, he could easily get **stranded** on a mudflat for hours. **Tidal streams** can also be a problem for boats trying to go against the flow. In places, tidal streams rush through narrow channels like rapids on a mountain river. These danger zones are called **rip tides.** Most boats avoid rip tides. But some people enjoy riding them for sport. It is a bit like white-water rafting. There is a boat crew here that takes people out to see what it is like. You join them on a trip.

White-knuckle ride

The crew use a high-powered inflatable speedboat, like the ones that are used by emergency services. You have to wear

a **personal flotation device,** just in case you get knocked off into the rough water. You strap on the device, climb onto the boat, and off you go. At first the boat races across fairly calm water. But then you see a headland, a point of land that juts out into the channel. You can see the water surging past the headland. It is three hours after low tide, and ocean water is pouring into the bay from the Atlantic Ocean. The boat speeds between

It takes a powerful boat to ride against the strongest tides. This inflatable boat is made stronger by a solid bottom.

the headland and a small island. Ahead of you the water is heaped up in high **stopper waves** that have white crests.

As you race into the channel with the engine roaring, the boat stops dead. It is perched on a stopper wave, which is rather like a waterfall. The water is pouring down beneath you in a great scoop. Then it surges up into another wave. The driver carefully increases the power. You creep forward over the foaming crest. Then the driver turns the boat on the next wave and you shoot back the way you came, down into the trough and over the top. Steering left, you swerve around the edge of a **whirlpool,** then up onto another stopper wave.

Eventually you head out into calmer water. You are exhausted and soaked, but now you know how powerful an ocean tide can be. You would only ever do this again with an experienced adult, though.

The waters around this rocky outcrop are very dangerous. The choppy, white area of the water shows where the rip tides occur.

Sea Power

The tall rocky pillars of Hopewell Rocks stand high above the low tide line. Some rocks have trees on top. At one time, all these rocks were part of the land.

While you are in the Bay of Fundy, you visit Hopewell Rocks on the New Brunswick shore. These rocks have been carved into strange shapes by the **tidal streams** that surge past them in both directions every day. The water picks up grains of sand that grind away the rock. This grinding, or **erosion,** produces more sand, and more erosion. Hopewell Rocks have been worn away where the water can reach them, and each one is now perched on a narrower stalk of rock. Eventually the rocks will fall into the sea.

High pressure

At Hopewell, most of the erosion has been caused by the huge **tides** in the Bay of Fundy. But storms do their bit as well. Storm waves are incredibly powerful. Great steel ships wrecked on the shore can be pounded to scrap within a few days. And when waves slam into a solid rock they can be just as destructive. Waves find their way into any cracks. The intense **pressure** can blow the rock apart.

It is very windy on the day you visit Hopewell Rocks. Since the wind has built up some big waves, you decide to check out a blowhole. This is where the waves force water into a hole in the rock. The pressure of the waves squeezes air and water out of a hole in the top of the cliff.

Your guide is a scientist who is studying coastal erosion. On a calm day she put a pressure **sensor** inside the blowhole. Luckily, the sensor is linked to a **digital display** by a long cable. That lets you read the pressure without getting too wet. Each big wave forces the pressure inside the blowhole up to an amazing 30 tons per square inch (4.7 metric tons per square centimeter). That is like having the whole weight of a school bus pressing down on one fingernail!

The spray of air and water from a blowhole is very powerful. It can be many feet high.

Tidal power plant

In the Annapolis Basin in the Bay of Fundy, the power of the tides is turned into electricity. Some of the huge weight of water that moves in and out every day is channeled through **turbines** linked to electrical generators. They can produce up to 20 megawatts of power. That is enough to run about 40,000 personal computers.

Wind and Waves

Your scientist friend lives near the rocky coast of the Gulf of Maine, south of the Bay of Fundy. She invites you to join him there. Together you are going to investigate rocky shores and the sea life that lives on them.

The **tides** in the Gulf of Maine are not huge like those in the Bay of Fundy. But the waves are bigger because the coast faces the open Atlantic Ocean. A wave that smashes against the shore here may have traveled 3,000 miles (4,800 kilometers) or more across the ocean. The farther a wave travels, the bigger it grows. Some of the waves in the Gulf of Maine are huge.

Atlantic storm

When you arrive, you get the chance to see these waves in action. There is a storm blowing toward the shore, and the waves are pounding the coast. You wrap up in your toughest waterproof clothes and go down to the bay to take a look.

The air is full of spray and the roar of breaking surf. It is nearly high tide. Up at the end of the bay the waves are smashing against the cliffs, with all the force you measured in the blowhole. The shore is also covered with big stones (cobbles) and boulders. The waves pick up the cobbles and hurl them against the cliffs. The stones help knock away bits of the rocky cliff. You can see where the waves have scooped caves out of the cliff face.

Gradually the waves cut the cliffs back. Where the rock is soft, this can happen at the rate of more than 3 feet (1 meter) a year. Tougher rocks are harder to wear away, or **erode.** But over thousands of years these wear away, too. Eventually the caves will collapse, and great masses of rock will fall into the sea.

All this happens only above the level of the waves. The rocks below sea level are often undamaged. Then, they form a wave-cut platform in front of the cliffs. Some platforms are almost flat, but the one in this bay is full of sloping cracks and crevices. When the tide goes down, it leaves the spaces between the rock ridges full of water. These rock pools are perfect places to look for the animals that live on rocky shores.

Adult acorn barnacles are safe in their tough shells at low tide. The barnacles feed at high tide when water covers them.

Even hard rocks in the tidal zone are worn away by the action of powerful waves.

Tidal Pools

The forecast for the next few days is storms and bad weather. You decide to visit a friend in California where the weather is fine. So you fly to San Francisco and head straight to the beach with your friend. Now, the weather is warm and sunny. It is also low **tide** at noon. This is an ideal day to explore the seashore. When you get down to the bay after breakfast, you find that the falling tide is slowly revealing a great stretch of rocky shore. The shore is dotted with rock pools. Near the top of the shore the rock is almost bare, so it is easy to jump from one rock to another. As you do, you look in the pools, but there is not a lot to see. Your scientist friend suggests that you check the water temperature and saltiness. You find that the pools are cool, and the salt content is the same as seawater. That is not much of a surprise.

Cold comfort

As you follow the falling tide down the shore the rocks get more difficult to walk on. They are covered with slippery green seaweed. There is also seaweed in the rock pools. When you look more closely you discover flowerlike sea anemones among the seaweed. There are also shrimp and small crabs. Barnacles, limpets, and small sea snails cling to the rocks. You cannot understand why these pools have more life in them than those higher up the shore.

This pool is on the lower shore. It is full of life because the water never gets hot.

The farther down the shore you go, the more wildlife you find. The rocks near the low tide line are covered with thick brown seaweed. And there are masses of mussels. The pools contain sea stars and hermit crabs that live inside the empty shells of sea snails. There are even small fish in the pools. The rock pools on the

lower shore support more wildlife than the pools on the upper shore. Why?

When you check the higher rock pools again, you find out. They have warmed up in the sunshine. A lot of the water has **evaporated.** The water that is left is now very salty. It is much too warm and salty for most sea life. But the lower pools are not exposed to direct sunlight for very long. They stay cool and comfortable until the tide rises again.

Two pink sea stars lie stranded on a mat of seaweed. If the tide returns too late they could dry out and die.

Monterey Bay Aquarium

You visit Monterey Bay Aquarium, in California, with your friend. There, you are able to see much of California's sealife up close. And you realize how the education program at the aquarium helps us understand about endangered animals, such as sea otters. Marine **biologists** are also able to study the aquarium's sea creatures.

Clammed Up

A lot of the animals and seaweeds you see on the beach seem able to survive out of the water. Most of these animals are tough shellfish, such as barnacles, limpets, and mussels. There are also sea anemones that have pulled their fleshy tentacles into their soft bodies and closed up like blobs of jello.

All these animals get their food and vital oxygen from the water. If they are left high and dry by the falling **tide,** they cannot eat or even breathe properly. They survive by closing up tight and sealing water inside their bodies. Then they wait for the tide to rise again.

Some are better at this than others. Mussels, for example, cannot survive out of the water for as long as barnacles. Mussels have to live closer to the low-tide line, so they are soon covered up when the tide comes back in. The barnacles can live farther up the shore.

Bands of life

As you look around the bay, you realize that the mussels, barnacles, and other wildlife form bands of different colors all along the shore. This striped effect is most obvious on the sheer cliffs. Your friend has a good way of getting a closer look. You are going to **rappel** from the top of the cliff.

Dangling from a rope, you work your way down the cliff face. Near the top there are tufts of grass and seaside flowers that can survive salt spray. Lower down in the **splash zone** there is a band of yellow lichen, and then a band of black lichen.

A sea anemone (left) with outstretched tentacles waits in a tidal pool, feeling for its next meal.

Lichen (below) survive in the splash zone because they can put up with the salty spray.

Rappelling

Rappelling is a way of using a rope to lower yourself down a sheer cliff. The rope is fixed at the top, and passes through a harness around your body. You can control how fast the rope runs through the harness, and even stop it altogether. You must not try this without an adult to help you.

Below this band there is a very pale brown zone where the rock is covered with barnacles. Below the barnacles, where it is wetter, there are dense beds of blue-black mussels. So the cliff is striped with yellow, black, pale brown, and blue-black, all around the headland. You have had a fun trip to the west coast, but now it is time to return east. The storms there have cleared. Your friend takes you to the airport, and you catch a plane to Boston.

On the Beach

After exploring the rocky shores of the Gulf of Maine and after your brief trip to California, you head for Cape Cod, near Boston. You want to see what happens to all the rock fragments that are carried away by the sea. You already know that they often end up on the beach. But maybe you did not know that beaches can grow just as fast as rocky shores are worn away.

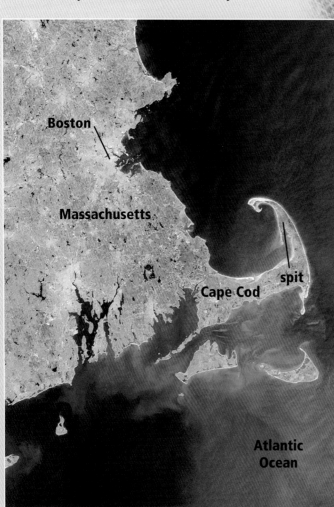

Boston

Massachusetts

Cape Cod

spit

Atlantic Ocean

Longshore drift

Where waves break on the shore at an angle, they push sand and stones sideways along the beach. This action is called longshore drift and can make long offshore spits. The spits may be covered at high tide, but they are exposed at low tide. Longshore drift has made the spits near Cape Cod.

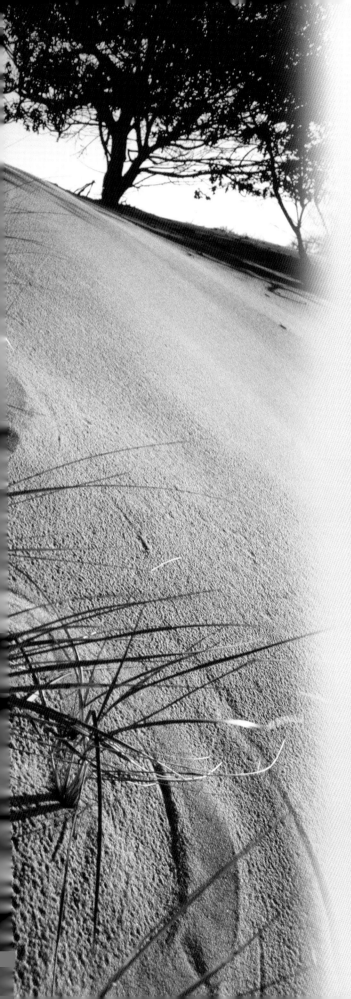

Wind has blown sand from the tidal zone into very big sand dunes on Cape Cod. Some of the dunes are 100 feet (33 meters) high.

Northern Cape Cod is just a huge beach. It has been built up over thousands of years by the ocean. The ocean **erodes** sand from the soft cliffs of southern Cape Cod, then dumps it on the shore and pushes it north in a process called longshore drift. Over time it has formed a long, curving **spit.** As the beach grows, the older parts farther from the sea become grassy. Then shrubs and trees grow on the spit. So, gradually the ocean creates new land. Sometimes a storm sweeps some of the land away, but the longshore drift builds it up again.

Back at the beach, you see where the wind has swept dry sand up into big sand dunes. Once, the oldest dunes were covered with oak and beech forests, but early European settlers cut down the trees. The soil blew away, leaving the sand. Dune grasses have been planted during the last 40 years. They help keep the sand from moving and allow trees to grow again.

Farther down the beach you step over the strand line, which is a long heap of debris dumped by the waves at high **tide.** You walk toward the ocean. The sand becomes much firmer because it is kept damp by the ocean. As you get closer to the water, you notice a lot of small hollows that show where marine worms and shellfish are buried. The wet sand looks empty, but it is obviously full of life.

Hidden Riches

The Cape Cod park authorities are doing some wildlife surveys on the beach, and you get the chance to help. As part of the project, the rangers are sampling small areas of the beach to find what is buried in the sand. You have already noticed some signs of buried animals. Now is your chance to discover what they are.

The rangers mark off a patch of sand low down on the beach, just 39 inches (1 meter) square, using a frame called a **quadrat.** By counting everything living in the square, they will be able to compare its **biodiversity,** or variety of life, with similar squares that have been sampled all over the world.

Then, you all start digging inside the quadrat. You must work fast, or some of the animals may escape. You pile the sand into tanks containing a little water. Some members of the team sift it through fine **sieves** to identify and count the animals.

Low life

It is surprising how many animals you find. There are big quahogs, which are a type of clam, and many small, pale, rounded clams called cockles. There are slimmer, more colorful clams called thin tellins and

---

*Edible cockles burrow into the sand when the **tide** is low. As the tide rises, these cockles are covered by water. That is when they filter food from the water.*

a few long, tubelike razor clams. The tellins suck pieces of food from the sand surface when the tide is in. Tellins use long tubes to suck with. Quahogs, cockles, and razor clams feed by drawing water down into their shells and eating any particles that they can. The razor clams have muscular "feet." The clams use these to drag themselves into the sand if a **predator** comes near.

Burrowing in the sand

You also find some marine worms. Many live in burrows and swallow the sand to digest any food in it. Others live in small protective tubes that they build from sand grains. The worms spread their tentacles

Coin-shaped sand dollars live in great numbers on beaches. They are often partly buried in the soft sand.

into the water to catch anything they can eat that might be drifting by. There are also burrowing sea urchin relatives called sand dollars. They plow through the sand, picking up any food particles they can find.

When the tide comes in, all these animals find plenty to eat in the sand or water. Bits of food are swept in by the waves. But when the tide goes out, the animals must lie low and wait for it to return again, just like the animals on rocky shores.

Mud and Marsh

On shores with big waves, very small mud particles in the water do not settle and form beaches. Only the bigger grains of sand settle. At Cape Cod, the sandy beaches are cut by channels that lead to stretches of quiet water inland. The **tides** make salt water flow in and out of these areas. But there are no big waves. Tiny particles are very light and do not settle out in rough waters. But the water is almost still, so the mud particles can settle here. Mud does not sound too interesting, but when the rangers take you to look at one of these quiet bays you find it is very beautiful. The mudflats that are exposed by the falling tide gleam in the Sun. You see hundreds of shorebirds walking on the mud. They look as though they are searching for food. But at first you cannot see what they are eating.

Marine worms live in the mud of tidal flats. There are more than 10,000 different kinds of marine worms.

Field microscope

A field **microscope** is designed to be used outside. It looks like a circular can, with an **eyepiece** on one side. It contains a **lens** system that can **magnify** an object up to 200 times. It lets you see all the tiny fragments in the mud.

When you look more closely you find that the mud is swarming with tiny snails. The rangers sample the mud for buried animals and find that it is full of clams and worms. There is far more life here than on the sandy beach. One of the rangers takes a sample of the mud itself, and you get to examine it under a field **microscope.** The mud sample is full of the remains of dead plants and animals. The buried worms and shellfish eat these dead **organisms.**

Salt marsh

At the edges of the mudflats, strange knobbly plants with no leaves grow from the mud. The stems of these plants contain a lot of fresh water. This helps them survive in a place where they are covered by salty sea water twice a day when the tide is high.

Since salt marshes are close to the shore they can be flooded by especially high tides, or when a strong storm breaks.

Farther up the shore, the mud is covered with tough grasses, sedges, and other plants that can survive living in salt water. The plants form a **salt marsh.** It is a wet wilderness between the land and the sea, full of shorebirds, crabs, and other animals.

Fuel Stop

The rangers do not just want to sample the animals living in the mud. They also want to check up on the shorebirds that are eating them. They have brought along a machine that shoots a net over a group of feeding birds. Then, they can examine the birds closely.

While the rangers are setting up the net, you watch the birds as they feed. You notice that some have longer legs than others. These birds often wade in the water instead of walking on the mud.

Some have short, stubby beaks and pick food from the mud surface. Others have longer beaks and probe deep into the mud for **prey.** You see a bird with a long, curved beak pull a worm from its burrow, and swallow it down. A ranger tells you the bird is a whimbrel. A few of the

Whimbrels love to eat burrowing crabs. The birds are careful to avoid mud that is too soft since it makes wading more difficult.

During a feeding session, terns hover above the water surface. When one sees a small fish below the waves it swoops down, grabs the fish, then swallows it.

wading birds are snatching things from the water surface. Just offshore, white birds with forked tails are diving into deeper water to catch fish. They are called terns.

Since each type of bird has a different feeding style, it eats different types of animals. This means that huge numbers of birds can feed on the same area of mud without running out of things to eat.

Arctic visitors

There are many birds feeding on this muddy area. So, when the rangers fire their net, they trap a lot of birds underneath it. This does not hurt the birds, but it helps the rangers find out

more about them. Some of the birds have metal bands on their legs, and the rangers check the writing on the bands. It tells them where the birds were banded and where they have come from.

It turns out that many of the banded birds have flown down from northern Canada, where they nested in the spring. It is now late summer, and the birds are flying south on **migration.** They will fly thousands of miles, all the way to South America. There, they will spend the winter. Cape Cod lies about half way along their journey, so they stop off to rest and feed.

The rich mudflats and **salt marshes** provide the birds with plenty of food, which they use as fuel for their long flight. They will stop off again on their return journey in spring. Then they will fly north again to the Canadian Arctic.

Seagrass Meadows

The plants that grow on **salt marshes** have to survive being flooded with salt water. But they spend at least part of every day in the open air. One group of flowering plants can live under the sea for almost all the time. These plants are called seagrasses.

You have been invited to join a group of students studying seagrass beds. The seagrass they are looking at is in the shallow coastal waters of a Caribbean island. It is a long way from Cape Cod, but you have a special reason for making the journey south.

Many Caribbean seagrass beds grow in white coral sand in sheltered bays and lagoons. The thick roots of the seagrass help keep the sand from moving during storms. Their long leaves provide shelter for all kinds of animals, including sea urchins, sea stars, crabs, lobsters, and fish such as seahorses.

Many of these creatures eat other animals, but two of the biggest—the green turtle and the manatee—feed on the seagrass itself. Manatees look like swimming pigs. They are slow-moving and eat plants, including the juicy roots of the seagrass.

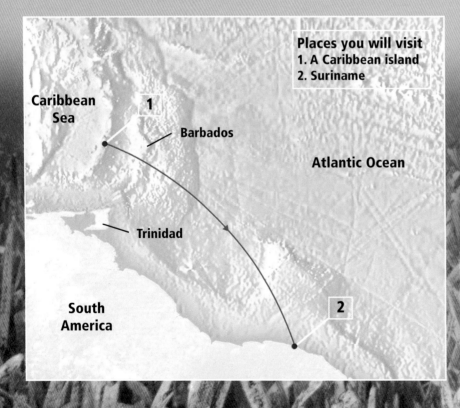

Places you will visit
1. A Caribbean island
2. Suriname

Caribbean Sea

1

Barbados

Atlantic Ocean

Trinidad

South America

2

Underwater vegetarians

Soon after you arrive, you get the chance to swim out and see manatees feeding in the shallow, crystal-clear water. They are digging in the sand with their broad snouts to get at the seagrass roots. Every few minutes, one of the manatees surfaces to take a noisy breath of air. When they surface, you see their tiny eyes and sensitive whiskers. They cannot see well, and they find their way mainly by touch and scent. One manatee swims up to you to investigate. It decides that you are harmless and goes back to its meal. That was an amazing experience. You are glad you came to the Caribbean.

Seagrass is a very important source of food for many different sea animals, including manatees.

Manatees in danger

Manatees have suffered badly from hunting, ocean pollution, and the destruction of their natural **habitats.** Manatees are often hit by powerboats, and injured by the boats' sharp propellers. The manatees that live on the coasts of Florida are now endangered. Their survival probably depends on the state wildlife parks, where their natural habitats are carefully preserved.

Turtle Nursery

During your stay with the students you see a lot of green sea turtles. They are feeding among the seagrass. Since the students have planned an expedition to one of the turtles' main breeding beaches on the South American shore, you are excited to go, too.

The beach is on a wild coast in Suriname, far from the nearest town. The female turtles mate with the males in the ocean. Then, they come ashore to lay their eggs in the beach sand. The site is carefully chosen so the sand and tide conditions are just right. Each female returns to the place where she was born. The turtles may use the same beach for thousands of years.

This female green sea turtle has found a good place to lay her eggs. She will use her flippers to dig in the soft sand. Then she will lay around 100 eggs.

Night visitor

It is near the end of the breeding season when you arrive. You have a chance of seeing hatching young as well as egg-laying turtles. You set up camp near the beach and wait for nightfall.

As the sky darkens, you see a big turtle coming ashore through the surf. She has spent nearly all her life in the water. It takes her a long time to haul herself up the sand to the **splash zone** above the highest tides. You watch her dig a hole in the sand with her flippers. Then she lays about 100 eggs before covering them up and heading back to the sea. The whole job has taken most of the night.

Meanwhile, the beach has come alive with scuttling ghost crabs. They are searching for food that has been washed up on the shore. But they like living **prey** as well. While the old turtle has been laying her eggs, baby turtles have been hatching from other nests on the beach. They are easy prey for the crabs.

The tiny turtles dig their way out of the sand and scuttle toward the sea. But only a few make it. Many are grabbed by the ghost crabs. Many more are snatched by the seabirds that fly to the beach at dawn. Yet some will survive, grow up, and eventually return to the same beach to lay their own eggs.

Ghost crabs spend most of their lives buried in sand dunes. The crabs breathe through **gills.**

Mangrove Swamp

The turtle nursery lies close to a quiet shore where the sea has dumped thick layers of mud. In cool New England, a muddy place like this would have become a **salt marsh** like the one you saw near Cape Cod. But here in the tropics it has become a mangrove swamp.

Mangroves are trees and bushes that are able to grow in **tidal** mud. Mangroves can form thick forests that look just like tropical rain forests from the air. But when you start to explore the mangroves, you find that they are very different.

Smart trees

For one thing, you need a boat to explore a mangrove forest. At high **tide** most of the forest is flooded. The trees seem to grow straight out of the sea. But as the tide goes down, the scene becomes even stranger. Some of the trees have weird roots that arch out from their trunks before disappearing into the mud. In other places the mud is crowded with wooden spikes and knobs.

When you dig down into the mud itself, you find that it smells strongly of rotten eggs. Yuk! It is waterlogged, airless, and very salty. All plants need to take up air, as well as water, through their roots. So it is surprising that the trees can grow here at all. But the arching roots of some

*Mangrove **seedlings** can only grow in calm waters on shallow, gently sloping shores.*

mangroves take in air from above the top of the mud. Other mangrove trees grow spikes and knobs from their roots that do the same thing.

Since mangrove roots are bathed in salty water, they suck up more salt than is good for the trees. The salt forms white **crystals** on their leaves. You pick a leaf and lick it. It tastes of the salt that you use on your food at home. The trees get rid of the salt they do not need through their leaves.

*The tangled roots of the mangrove trees provide a safe home for many animals. There, they are protected from **predators.***

You wonder how these trees grow, since it seems impossible that their seeds could sprout in the tidal mud. Yet when you look around you see baby trees. You look up. Above you there are tiny plants sprouting from seeds that are still fixed to a branch. They fall off, drift away in the water, then start growing somewhere else.

37

Mangrove Life

This scarlet ibis gets its vivid
red color from chemicals
in the tiny animals it eats.

Exploring the mangrove swamp is not very pleasant. You are surrounded by swarms of biting mosquitoes. And spiders seem to have built their webs everywhere. The branches of the mangroves are crawling with ants. But all these small animals provide food for lizards and small birds. The lizards and birds attract **predators** like snakes and eagles.

As you paddle your boat through the forest at high **tide,** you see a flock of dazzling scarlet ibis perched up in the trees. In another tree, big fruit bats are hanging upside down from the branches. They look like badly folded umbrellas.

The water is alive, too. When you collect a sample and look at it closely, you discover that it is full of tiny fish. Some may spend their lives here, but many are the young of ocean fish such as marlin. The tangle of mangrove roots protects them from bigger fish that might eat them. When they are big enough, the fish move out into the open sea. Mangroves protect many coral **reef** fish while they are growing up.

Fiddler crabs

When the tide flows away, the mud comes alive with fiddler crabs. Most crabs live underwater. There, they use their **gills** to take in oxygen from the water. Fiddler crabs and ghost crabs need to keep their gills wet to breathe. So they have to return to the water sometimes. But the rest of the time they can look for food on mudflats and beaches.

A male fiddler crab has one huge, brightly colored claw that he uses for fighting and showing off to females. He uses his other claw to sort through the mud for tiny bits of food. A female fiddler crab picks up food with two claws, so she can feed twice as quickly! Fiddler crabs feed only when the mud is exposed at low tide, be it day or night.

After it gets dark, you return to the mangroves. There are hundreds of crabs feeding on the mud. You can also hear bigger animals moving through the forest. The forest feels very eerie, and you decide that it is time to move on.

Fish that climb trees

Strange little fish called mudskippers live in the mangrove swamps of the tropical Pacific and Indian Oceans. Mudskippers are able to live out of the water like fiddler crabs do. Mudskippers use their fins to hop around on the mud. They can even climb trees!

A Breeding Beach

After your visit to the mangrove swamp in Suriname, you fly to southern South America. There, it is summer. You head for the beaches where southern sea lions breed.

Seals, sea lions, whales, and dolphins are air-breathing **mammals,** like us. But while whales and dolphins do not leave the sea, seals and sea lions come back to the shore to **mate** and have their babies.

These animals need quiet **tidal** shores. When you arrive at the Valdés Peninsula in Argentina, you find thousands of seals and sea lions on the stony beach. Many of the female sea lions have given birth to their pups. They are feeding them with their rich milk. The sea lions are not afraid of you and your guide. You can even walk among them taking photographs.

You are not the only visitors to the sea lion beach. There are a lot of seabirds called giant petrels. They feed on dead sea lion pups and other bits of food lying on the

A sea lion colony can be overcrowded. Each powerful male sea lion is in charge of several females. If another male tries to take control, there will probably be a fight.

ground. Beaches where sea lions breed offer rich pickings for **scavengers,** such as giant petrels and foxes.

Beach fight

While the female sea lions are looking after their pups, the much bigger males have other things on their minds. They compete with each other to mate with the females after the females have given birth to their pups. You are just about to take a great photograph of a sea lion pup when a fight breaks out nearby. The rival sea lions rear up face to face. They roar and grunt as they try to bite each other. It is soon obvious that one male sea lion is winning. You stand well back as the other male turns around and lumbers away with blood streaming from its wounds. The sea lion only just misses crushing a pup. It is just as well that you moved away!

You have already seen a giant petrel feasting on one dead pup that might have been killed like this. It seems like the sea lions might be their own worst enemies. But then you meet an animal that makes even the biggest sea lion look tame.

Orca Attack!

A little farther down the coast, some of the sea lions are swimming in shallow water just off the pebble beach. Your guide has brought you here to see another kind of sea **mammal.** It usually stays away from the shore. But here it comes right into the shallows, and even on to the beach, for a reason. This is surprising because it is as big as a truck and weighs as much as 30 male sea lions. It is a killer whale, or orca.

Orcas kill and eat sea lions swimming in the sea. Here on the Valdés Peninsula they have also learned to catch their **prey** in the tidal zone. The orcas are most active later in the summer when the sea lion pups are old enough to swim. But one of the orcas is hunting already.

You sit on the pebbles, well clear of the water, and watch. The sea lions seem to be enjoying themselves. They swim, dive, and bob in the waves, just like weekenders on a California beach. They make a pretty sight, but after nearly an hour you are getting bored. You are watching the birds instead, when your guide tugs your arm.

Deadly giant

Out in the blue water, a tall black fin is plowing toward the beach. It is an orca. It turns slightly and aims directly at the sea lions. They see it coming and head for the beach, but they are too late.

*Orcas risk being stranded
when they attack sea lions
in the tidal zone.*

The orca surges forward, pushing up a very large wave of water. The orca seizes one of the sea lions in its teeth.

The sea lion looks tiny as it struggles to get free. The giant whale smacks it against the beach until it goes limp. Meanwhile, the killer has got stuck on the beach. It has to waddle and flap its great body to get back into the water. Then the orca slides away, back into the ocean. You feel safe again.

Beached whales

Whales of various kinds often get **stranded** on beaches by accident. No one knows why. A stranded whale cannot survive for long on shore. If it cannot get back into the ocean, it dies. Without water to support its weight, its lungs are crushed. When it is dead, it makes a feast for all kinds of **scavenging** animals, from crabs and seabirds to bears and wolves.

Mission Debriefing

Your exploration of the tidal zone has taken you all the way down the western fringes of the Atlantic Ocean. You traveled from the cold harbors of Nova Scotia to the rocky shores of California and the tropical beaches of the Caribbean, then to the cold southern shores of Argentina. You saw a variety of habitats and animals, but some things stayed the same.

On every shore that you visited, the rising and falling **tide** created a shifting border between the land and the ocean. This area is rich in food, swept in from the ocean and off the land. But only a few types of animals are able to enjoy this food, because life in the tidal zone is so difficult. The animals have to survive battering waves, tumbling rocks, shifting sands, and tides that leave them high and dry twice a day.

Yet some types of animals can survive. And because there is so much food, they survive in huge numbers. A rocky headland may be home to millions of barnacles, and a muddy beach conceals billions of marine worms. Despite everything, the tidal zone is one of richest parts of the ocean.

These colorful sea stars and sea anemones are in the tidal zone on a California beach.

Glossary

biodiversity variety of life in any area

biologists people who study animals and plants

crystals gemlike structures formed naturally by substances such as salt and rock minerals

digital display electronic show of data in the form of numbers

erode wear away rock or other materials

erosion the process of wearing away rock or other materials by waves, rivers, or the wind

evaporate turn to vapor, or gas. When water turns to water vapor it is evaporating.

eyepiece part of a microscope or similar device that you hold to your eye

gill blood-filled organ that fish and other animals use to absorb oxygen from the water

gravity force of attraction that pulls things toward planets and moons

habitat place that provides the right food, shelter, and other needs for animals

lens piece of curved glass that bends light and makes things look bigger or smaller

magnify make something look bigger

mammal warm-blooded, often furry animal that feeds its young on milk

mate when males and females come together to makes eggs or young

microscope tool for looking at things too small to see with the naked eye

migration regular journey, usually over a long distance

orbit travel around a star, planet, or moon in space

organism living thing. All plants and animals are organisms.

personal flotation device airfilled jacket or collar that keeps you afloat in an emergency

predator animal that hunts, kills, and eats other animals

pressure squeezing or pushing force

prey animal that is killed and eaten by other animals

quadrat frame used by scientists to mark a small area of ground for sampling

rappel use a rope to make a controlled descent down a rock face

reef area of rock or rocky coral that sticks up from the seafloor

rip tide fast tidal flow that can cause dangerous currents and waves

salometer device that measures the saltiness of water

salt marsh grassy swamp that forms on a mudflat in cool salt water

scavenger animal that eats the remains of dead things. Scavenging animals feed this way.

seedling a very young plant, such as a baby tree

sensor device that measures things, such as water pressure and temperature

sieve device with holes that filters out larger organisms or pieces of mud and sand

spit beach that extends out into the water, away from the land

splash zone part of the shore above the high tide line that is splashed by salt water

stopper wave wave that stays in one place, formed by fast currents flowing over rocks

stranded stuck on the shore by the falling tide

tidal stream sideways flow of water created by a rising or falling tide

tide local rise and fall in sea level. Tidal shores are those affected by tides.

tide range difference in height between high and low tide

turbine fanlike device that rotates when liquid or gas flows through it

whirlpool a very fast current of water that spins around and around

Further Reading and Websites

Books

Earle, Sylvia. *National Geographic Atlas of the Ocean: The Deep Frontier.* Washington, D.C.: National Geographic Society, 2001.

Laskey, Elizabeth. *Sea Turtles.* Chicago: Heinemann Library, 2003.

Nadeau, Isaac. *Food Chains in a Tide Pool Habitat.* New York: Rosen Publishing Group, Inc., 2001.

Websites

www.bbc.co.uk/nature/blueplanet
The website of the BBC series about ocean life, with extra information and games.

www.homesafe.com/manatee/
A website for manatee enthusiasts, giving information, stories, photographs, and links to other manatee websites.

http://www.nps.gov/caco/
All about the Cape Cod National Seashore, with photographs and information about its geography and wildlife.

oceanexplorer.noaa.gov
The website of the US National Oceanic and Atmospheric Administration, about the technology of ocean exploration and ocean wildlife.

www.seasky.org/sea.html
A website packed with information about the ocean.

www.valleyweb.com/fundytides/
All about the enormous tides in the Bay of Fundy, and the best places to go to see their effects.

Index